sports 'n' all

"There is a tendency with television for people to just sit there with feet up, eating pizza and drinking beer and that is their participation in sports. I don't think that is bad."

Richard Nixon 37th President of the USA

First published in Great Britain in 1997 by
Chameleon Books
106 Great Russell Street
London WC1B 3LJ

CIP data for this title is available from the British Library

ISBN 0 233 99181 6

Jacket design by Generation Studio. Book design by Ian Hammond.

Printed in Spain by G.Z. Printek

Andre Deutsch Ltd is a subsidiary of VCI plc

ACKNOWLEDGEMENTS:

Special thanks to Mike Wood, Paul Sudbury,
Mary Killingworth, Mark Peacock, Joanne Meeks,
all at Generation Associates, all keen sports fans across
the country and the man who made it all possible -
Tim Forrester.

A special thanks to Adrian Murrell
and the lads at Allsport.

Dedicated to
Caroline Warde

Richard Burton, the incomparable actor, could have played Rugby for Wales as a wing-forward, if he had not succumbed to the lure of footlights and Shakespeare and Hollywood Producers with dollar accents. Richard himself claimed that "I was born slightly off-side and always crossed on the amber light" - the perfect qualities for a breakaway forward.

He also swore that a man from Llanelli cured his shingles by touching the boot of Barry John when it was charged with miracles after he had kicked six goals against England!

There are, in the world of sport, massive lies and stupendous exaggerations and it is on their stories that the richness and the complexities of life are created. The stories and insight and the enrichment of the spirit, spell out sport at it's very best, for it is gladiatorial adventure we all yearn for toughness, style, fair play and laughter.

The writer, Hugh McIllvaney, often claim's that sport is a nonsense - a very important nonsense - but still a nonsense.

In a fumbling, highly professional world of sport, amen to that.

Cliff Morgan

6

OLD SPORTSMEN NEVER DIE

THE ORIGINS OF SPORTS can be traced back to ancient Egyptian or Greek times. Coursing was believed to have taken place in Egypt as early as 3000 BC. Wrestling took place in what is now Iraq more than 4,000 years ago; a form of hockey was played in Egypt about 2050 BC; and boxing, track and field athletics, and fencing are other sports to have been played more than 4,000 years ago.

"I am a great golfer. I just haven't played the game yet."
MUHAMMAD ALI

STRUCK OUT

AMANDA GUILD probably regretted her prowess at tenpin bowling. Named the bowler of the week by a Michigan newspaper, her picture was recognised by police. Guild had fled drugs charges in Tennessee, but was re-arrested before her next game.

GLAM GIRL

TOP BRITISH ARCHER Alison Williamson decided to pose topless for Esquire magazine saying: "There is not much glamour in archery. If we receive publicity as a result it will have been worthwhile."

"Why didn't you just belt it?"
BARBARA SOUTHGATE, GARETH'S MUM.

"I've had it. If anyone sees me near a boat they can shoot me."
QUADRUPLE OLYMPIC ROWING GOLD MEDALLIST STEVE REDGRAVE.

WG IN A HURRY

WG GRACE is widely held as the greatest cricketer who ever lived, but he had other strings to his bow, as well. In 1866, playing against Surrey he scored 224 not out over the course of two days. He then proceeded to win the 440 yard hurdles race at the first National Olympian Association meeting which was held at Crystal Palace.

HE CUT THROUGH THE FIELD LIKE A KNIFE

HERO OF THE 1964 OLYMPICS was probably Ethiopian marathon runner Abebe Bikila, who with just five weeks to go before the big race, underwent an operation for appendicitis. He resumed training just three weeks before the day of the marathon, which he won by a margin of four minutes.

'When you're as great as I am it's hard to be humble.'

MUHAMMAD ALI

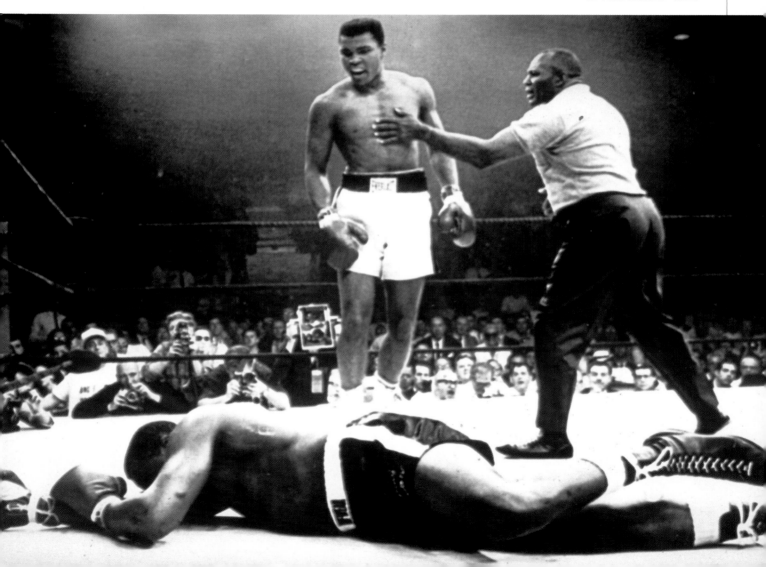

There's more than 50,000 out there - one of them must come from Manchester.

11

LAME EXCUSE

MANCHESTER UNITED offered one of football's most bizarre excuses for losing a game. On the way to losing 3-1 at Southampton, the Utd team changed their shirts from grey to blue and white at half time as they were having trouble seeing each other.

FLASHY

PATRICK DECKERS, a midfield player with Dutch team Eindhoven, found himself sacked by the club following a flashing incident. Deckers was sent off during a match against Helmond Sport, and on his way off the pitch he dropped his shorts and paraded his privates to the crowd. An Eindhoven official commented: "Showing ones' genitals in public is forbidden by law."

Players auditioning for the new Eric Cantona film, "I'm sick as a sea-gull now that the fat lady's singing."

UNLUCKY

PITY POOR ROBERT ULLATHORNE. One of the memories he left etched on the minds of Norwich City fans was his farcical own goal to gift the game to local rivals Ipswich Town. A gentle back pass to keeper Bryan Gunn trickled over the stricken goalie's foot as it hit a divot of turf and bounced up and eventually into the net. Ullathorne moved on to Spain, and then was brought back to English soccer by Leicester City. Pitched into a Coca Cola semi final against Wimbledon for his debut, Ullathorne was stretchered off with a broken foot after just 12 minutes. Curiously, there were no other players around him when he went down.

> ‘ Football, in itself, is a grand game for developing a lad physically and also morally, for he learns to play with good temper and unselfishness, to play in his place, and ‘play the game’ and these are the best of training for any game of life. ’
>
> LORD BADEN POWELL.

THE JUGGLER SACKED

BARRY FRY certainly kept himself busy during his two and a half year tenure as manager of Birmingham City. He masterminded no less than 55 incoming transfers to the club, but with a keen eye for balancing the books, he also managed to offload a total of 56 players.

REDS TAKE A TUMBLE

FA CUP UPSET IN 1984 as Bournemouth beat Manchester Utd, at the time second in Division 1. The Utd team contained the likes of Wilkins, Robson, Muhren and Whiteside and were managed by Ron Atkinson. Big Ron said later of the defeat: "It was a horrible experience. Funnily enough, we beat Barcelona not long after in the Cup Winners' Cup and I told Maradona he could think himself lucky he wasn't playing Bournemouth."

ONLY JOKING

NOTTINGHAM FOREST STRIKER JASON LEE requested a transfer following a major loss of form which he curiously attributed to being made the constant butt of jokes from TV comedians Frank Skinner and David Baddiel. The comedy duo had started poking fun at Lee's pineapple head haircut, and fans had picked up on the phrase and turned it into a chant directed at Lee whenever he touched the ball.

SEND IN THE CLOWN

THE 17TH OCTOBER 1973 is a date etched in the history of English international football. Playing Poland at Wembley in a World Cup Qualifier, England were confident of getting the win that would see them through to the Finals. "England will murder them" said the Daily Express banner headline, and they did, but they couldn't get the ball past goalkeeper Jan Tomaszewski, unkindly labelled "a clown" by none other than Brian Clough. A 1-1 draw meant it was the Poles who went to the Finals while the three lions licked their wounds.

ANYONE FOR CHICKEN?

GRIMSBY'S ITALIAN STAR import Ivano Bonetti falls out with his boss Brian Laws in a big fashion after a match. The incident culminates in Bonetti needing hospital treatment for a fractured cheekbone and cuts. A plate of chicken is the only other casualty in the dressing room fracas.

I USED TO BE FORGETFUL...

ASSISTANT REFEREE GRAEME THORLEY looked a bit of a charlie when he arrived to run the line for the Middlesex Senior Cup quarter final between Wembley and Edgware Town in February 1997. Thorley didn't manage to turn up until halfway through the 1st half - he had totally forgotten about the game. Fortunately, sports editor of the Harrow Observer, John Comfort, a qualified referee, was on hand to step in and deputise.

"It was very enjoyable," he told his own newspaper. "Particularly as I was running the line on the side where Edgware manager, Jack McGleish, was standing. His customary advice was greatly appreciated."

NOT VERY CLEVER

THE LAST FEW GAMES OF A FOOTBALL SEASON are always a tense affair, especially where relegation is concerned. But Manchester City manager Alan Ball did his team no favours at all in their last game of the 95/96 season as they stood on the brink of the drop. Holding Liverpool 2-2 at Maine Road, Ball believed a draw was enough as fellow strugglers Southampton were losing. He got a message to his players on the park saying as much, unfortunately he got his maths wrong - and Man City went down.

> **"You don't score 64 goals in 86 games at the highest level without being able to score goals."**
> ALAN GREEN, RADIO 5 LIVE.

‘ If a fox is completely
brilliant he finds a hole
and hides.
If he's discovered,
he's dug up and
thrown to the hounds.
But a football manager
hasn't even got
a hole to hide in. ’

BRIAN CLOUGH

GONE FISHIN'

A GOLFER IN NEWARK once struck a ball into a river. To his surprise, up floated a 2lb trout, killed by the errant shot.

"I win because I don't often have punctures."
CYCLING GREAT BERNARD HINAULT

"I'd like to thank Embassy but unfortunately I don't smoke."
STEVE DAVIS AFTER WINNING THE 1981 EMBASSY WORLD SNOOKER CHAMPIONSHIP.

KISS MY ...

BOULES is a big sport in France, and it is customary for each club to have a doll or a model of a buxom lady ensconced in the clubhouse with the specific purpose of humiliating players. If a team fails to register a point during a match, then each member of that team must kneel and kiss the doll's backside. This particular ritual is known as "Fanny".

NOT A GOOD DAY

JANE GOODAY withdrew from the Scottish Bowls Championships because she was taking banned substances. But you could forgive her, she was 73 and taking diuretics for a heart condition. None of her team was actually younger than 50, and she said afterwards: "Most of us take drugs for something, half the club will have to be banned."

"When Jack Nicklaus told me I was playing Seve in the singles I took so many pills I was mighty glad they didn't have drug tests for golfers."
GOLFER FUZZY ZOELLER ABOUT THE RYDER CUP IN 1983

SPIKED ARROWS

THE FORTYNINE CLUB OF CAERPHILLY had trouble concentrating during an away match. The team's cakes had been spiked with a hallucinogenic drug and the match turned into chaos as the majority of the Fortyniners were carted away for medical attention. Barmaid at the match venue, Emma Cannon, said: "It took four ambulances to get them all to hospital. There were only four of the away team left at the end. Apparently they didn't eat the cakes as they were dieting."

**It's okay,
I don't think the
photographer
can see where
my hand is.**

WHAT'S IT ALL ABOUT FRANK?

TV COMMENTATOR FRANK BOUGH was thrown in at the deep end for his first Olympics, the 1964 Tokyo games. He was asked to commentate on the Greco-Roman wrestling, a sport which he not surprisingly knew nothing about. The following conversation took place between Bough and his cameraman, Roy Gladish, as the action slowed down:

Bough: "Roy!"

Gladish: "Yup!"

Bough: "Roy, do you, er , reckon they've finished, Roy?"

Gladish: "Yup. I reckon they've finished."

Bough: "Roy?"

Gladish: "Yup?"

Bough: "Roy, who do you reckon won, Roy?"

Gladish: "I'm buggered if I know!"

(FROM "CUE FRANK" BY FRANK BOUGH)

> **"Having a mohawk is great. It works like a helmet and it's a great sundial because if I stand in a certain position I can tell the time with it. Mind you, if there's a stray crosswind, I tend to get blown off."**
> IRON MAN COMPETITOR
> CHUCKIE VEYLUPEK ON
> HIS PUNK HAIRDO

MISSED THE POST

TURKEY collected four gold medals in freestyle wrestling at the 1948 Olympics, but the golden quartet of athletes were unable to defend their titles at the 1952 games as officials forgot to put their entries in the post.

"Rosenborg have won 66 games, and they've scored in all of them."
BRIAN MOORE, ITV.

"Boxing is just show business with blood."
FRANK BRUNO

❝Professional wrestling's most mysterious hold is on its audience.❞
LUKE NEELY

FOR QUEEN AND COUNTRY

IN THE 1997 FIVE NATIONS, England beat Ireland in Dublin by a record score of 46-6. The Guardian wrote: "Could England's literal whitewash have been anything to do with the playing of God Save The Queen before a Dublin international for the first time since independence in 1921?

It used to be played when Ireland ran out at Ravenhill in Belfast. At the last match there in 1954, seven of the 15 who had travelled from the south, including the Reverend Robin Roe, a Church of Ireland Chaplain in the British Army, threatened to stay in the changing room until the brass band homage to a foreign monarch had finished. So it was not played - and the Irish Rugby Union at the time offered the excuse that the silence had been 'out of respect for Pope Pius XII, who was very ill at the time."

MIND YOUR LANGUAGE

THE ENGLAND V WALES MATCH at Twickenham in 1927 was the first team game in Britain to be broadcast with radio commentary. The man behind the microphone was Captain HBT Wakelam, who was not given too much help from his BBC employers about this brand new medium of reporting. The only advice he received was a note stuck near his microphone saying "Don't Swear!"

WHO'S THE NICE MAN IN THE BLACK?

WOLVERHAMPTON POLYTECHNIC OLD BOYS made a name for themselves at the 1996 Hong Kong Carlsberg 10s tournament. In their quarter final match against Tokyo Gaijiin, the former students found themselves up against a far superior 10s team, and consequently the points were rattling up in favour of the Tokyo side but none for Wolves. Until the Irish referee took pity and awarded the students a penalty try for persistent Tokyo infringement. Wolves fly half John Corr then requested that the ref took the conversion, which he duly drop kicked neatly through the middle of the posts. Thus in the match Wolverhampton totalled seven points without one of their players scoring.

SOFT EXCUSE

DAVID SOLE, a stalwart for Scotland at prop forward and a former captain of the national side, failed to turn up for a disciplinary hearing in 1995 because, he explained, he had to babysit.

LEAGUE LEADERS

THE DEBATE about which code produces the better team, League or Union, was effectively settled in 1996 with a clash between League's Wigan and Union's Bath. A two leg affair saw Wigan win the league version 82-6 and Bath win the union match 44-19. However, Wigan also romped home in the Middlesex 7s tournament, putting more experienced sides to shame.

> "I thought I would have a quiet pint… followed by about 17 noisy ones."
>
> GARETH CHILCOTT PLANS HIS RETIREMENT PARTY FROM BATH RUFC.

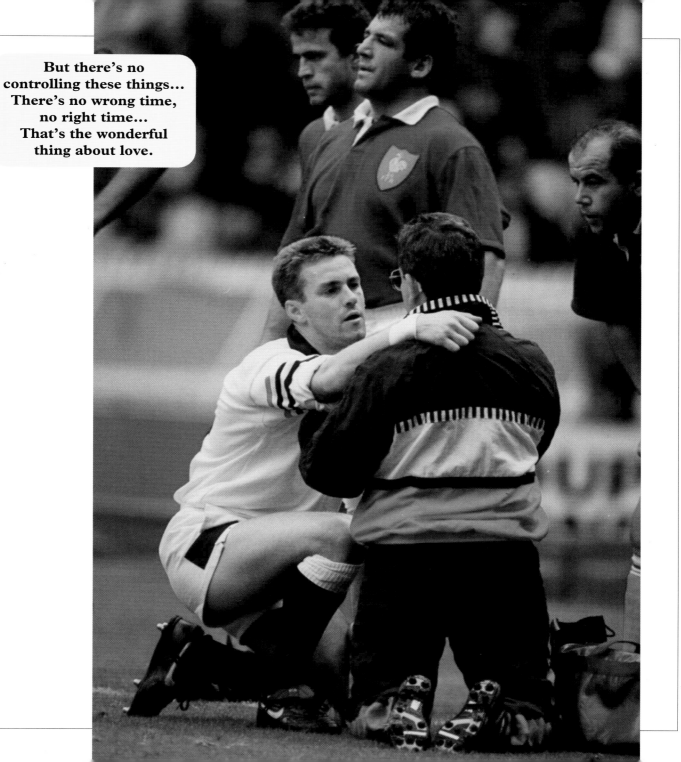

TWO GRAND A YARD

ROBERT ALLENBY hit just one shot in the 1996 Volvo Masters, a tee shot which travelled barely 40 yards, before pulling out of the event. Still recovering from a broken sternum suffered in a car accident, the Australian golfer turned up at Valderrama for the tournament to secure a £75,000 bonus (which he donated to charity) and more importantly, his position in the Order of Merit.

At my age, when your eyesight starts to go, you need much bigger knitting needles.

"He told me that he used to play for just twenty pounds a week. Today he would be worth all the money in the Bank of England."
ZOLA ON
SIR STANLEY MATTHEWS

"If Jack Nicklaus had to play my tee shots, he couldn't break 80. He'd be a pharmacist with a string of drugstores in Ohio."
LEE TREVINO

"Being an ex-England manager, one that failed to qualify for the World Cup, is like being a dead politician."
GRAHAM TAYLOR

AMERICAN FOOTBALL

WRONG TURNING

MINNESOTA VIKINGS' JIM MARSHALL saw the opportunity for glory in 1964 when he pounced on a fumble by the San Francisco 49ers. Marshall scooped up the ball, and completed a 66-yard rumble up the pitch and into the end-zone. Unfortunately, it was his own end-zone as he had headed off in the wrong direction. Instead of a 6-point touchdown he conceded a 2-point safety for the 49ers.

GET OJ!

IT IS A PECULIARITY OF AMERICAN FOOTBALL that the worst team of the season gets the first pick of the next season's college draft of players. The 1968 season was a particularly tense battle of the no-hopers, because shining like a beacon among the college wannabes was one OJ Simpson, already picked out as a legend in the making. Philadelphia Eagles found themselves best placed to win the race for last place, and therefore for Simpson, but having not won all season, the Eagles somehow contrived to win two of their last three games and that let in the Buffalo Bills, who duly signed OJ. It was a no win situation for Eagles coach Joe Kuharich, because when he finally got his team winning, the fans called for his head for depriving them of Simpson for the following season.

YOU STINK

THE ATLANTA FALCONS were dreadful in the 1974 season, and their fans told them so. A December game against Green Bay Packers was notable for the fact that 48,830 Atlanta fans bought tickets and then failed to turn up to watch.

HISTORY REPEATS

How could we live without instant replay today? The first replay to be shown was in the USA in 1963 during the Army V Navy American Football match. The action repeated was a touchdown by Army, accompanied by the shouted commentary of Lindsey Nelson: "This is not live! Ladies and gentlemen, Army did not score again."

**Listen fatboy;
this is a football game.
Go sing somewhere else.**

**"Trying to maintain
order during a legalised
gang brawl involving 80
toughs with a little
whistle, a hanky and a ton
of prayer."**

**How an American
Football NFL referee
described his job.**

O.K. SIMMONS,
If he says "pretty please"
will you give him his
helmet back?

Rugby is a beastly
game played by
gentlemen. Soccer is a
gentlemen's game played
by beasts. American
Football is a beastly game
played by beasts.

HARRY BLAHA

My idea of a good hit is when the victim wakes up on the sidelines with train whistles blowing in his head. I like to believe that my best hits border on felonious assault.

JACK TATUM

American football makes rugby look like a Tupperware party.

SUE LAWLEY.

Heads! I win.

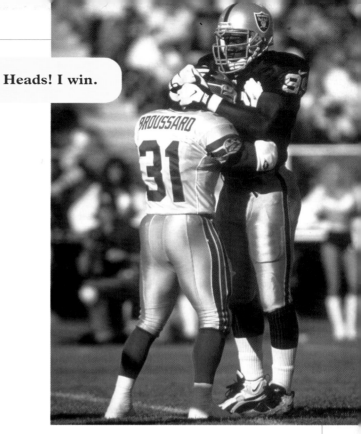

Hey man, are you wearing a protective box or are you just glad to see me?

LEGS CROSSED

IN JANUARY OF 1996 Southampton and Crewe had to postpone their FA Cup clash due to a lack of adequate toilet facilities.

NO CARE FOR BEAR

FANS OF BEAR BAITING included members of the Royal Family, namely Henry VIII and Elizabeth I. Moves to ban the sport were finally successful in 1835 but the premise of the ban was "not because it gave pain to the bear, but because it gave pleasure to the spectators."

BEEF FOR DINNER

IN 1934, the club professional at St Margaret's-at-Cliffe Golf Club in Kent, WJ Robinson, drove off the 18th tee and managed to kill a cow, which was standing some 100 yards away. The ball struck the cow square on the back of the head, and she was dead by the time the golfers reached her.

NEVER MIND, EH?

SIXTY FIVE YEAR OLD Paul Cerutti of Monaco was disqualified from the 1976 Olympic trap shooting event for drug usage. Even under the influence, though, he only managed to finish 43rd out of 44 competitors.

IT'S ONLY A GAME

SO TENSE was a 1970 World Cup game between El Salvador and Honduras that it led to a few sparks flying. More than a few, really, it actually kicked off a three day war between the two countries.

IN THE OLD DAYS

A form of football was played in China over 2,500 years ago.

"The FA Cup can be very romantic. But not for us."
MIDDLESBOROUGH BOSS BRUCE RIOCH AFTER CUP DEFEAT AT HOME TO GRIMSBY IN 1989.

"We didn't lose on the pitch - we lost away from it."
JUNINHO'S F.A. CUP VERDICT.

"I am going back to Italy and I will be keeping my mobile phone switched on."
GUIANLUCA FESTA AFTER CHELSEA'S 2-0 FA CUP WIN

**Pardon me!
I've just done a
bottom burp**

ENTITLED TO AN OPINION

NOTTINGHAM PANTHERS sacked their stadium organist after he played Send In The Clowns to greet the officials on to the ice, and then followed up with Three Blind Mice when they left the rink.

BUGGED

EAST GERMAN BEAUTY Katarina Witt was apparently bugged by the secret police even when she was having sex.

ICE TEE

SCOTT BASE COUNTRY CLUB is the most southerly golf course in the world, located just 13 degrees north of the South Pole. Full survival kit is needed to play, and instead of bunkers and water, natural hazards include penguins, seals and skuas. A one shot penalty is applied if a ball is stolen by a skua, but a birdie can be marked on the card if a player manages to hit one.

> **"There's nobody fitter at his age, except maybe Raquel Welch."**
> RON ATKINSON PAYS TRIBUTE TO GORDON STRACHAN.

Here I am boys!

EQUAL OPPORTUNITIES

WOMEN were allowed to play in the World Darts Championship for the first time in 1995. Deta Hedman made the most progress, beating two male competitors before losing in the third round.

NO WOMEN AND NO KIT

THE OLYMPIC GAMES as a sporting contest were originally held in Olympia, a city in ancient Greece, every four years during a sacred truce. Women were forbidden to be present at the games, and the male contestants competed in the nude. These ancient Games were abolished AD 394.

ALWAYS THE BRIDESMAID

AT every Olympic Games betwen 1936 and 1960, a British athlete won the silver medal in the women's high jump - but never the gold.

> "I try to keep my bra on at all times."
>
> HOW DAMON HILL'S WIFE GEORGIE AVOIDS BEING A DISTRACTION IN THE PIT LANE.

GOOD SPORT

IN the 1896 Olympic 100km cycling race, Frenchman Leon Flameng led the only other competitor, a Greek cyclist, by a huge distance. Such was Flameng's sense of sporting etiquette, however, that when the Greek rider's cycle broke down, Flameng dismounted and waited for the repairs to be carried out. Once the Greek rider was back in the saddle, Flameng carried on to win by six laps.

These mountain bikes <u>are</u> good.

39

I'm gonna break
your ankle if you
don't submit

What a load
of bollocks

41

**Never starch
your jock strap**

EAT THOSE WORDS

TONY GREIG, South African born former England captain probably had good cause to regret his promise to make the 1976 touring West Indian team "grovel". The West Indies, and a young Viv Richards, in particular, took exception to the remarks and thumped England 3 - 0 in the Test Series. Richards scored a total of 829 runs in the four Tests he took part in.

ROBO GOLFER

SO GOOD was Byron Nelson as a golfer, an equipment manufacturer designed a robot to hit golf balls in its research department, and modelled the robot's swing on that of Nelson. The machine was nicknamed Iron Byron. Nelson holds a record which is unlikely to be broken - in the 1945 season he won 11 professional tournaments in a row.

"Fred sent me to see if I could spot
a weakness, and I found one.
The half-time tea's too milky."
SHREWSBURY COACH
KEVIN SUMMERFIELD'S REPORT
ON HIS SPYING TRIP TO
FA CUP OPPONENTS LIVERPOOL.

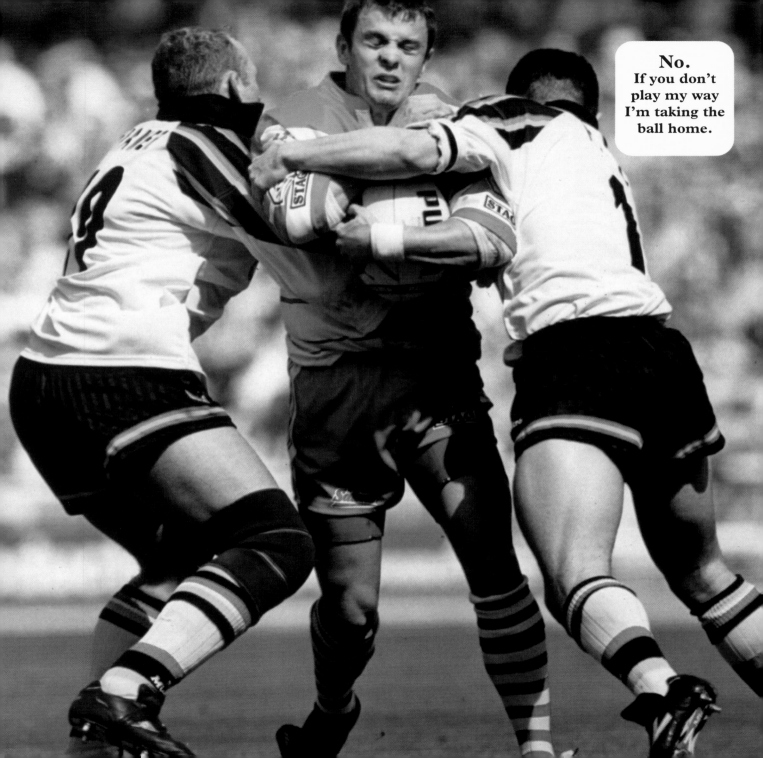

ROUND OF APPLAUSE

CLIVE LLOYD'S last first class game was, fittingly enough, a Lords final. When the tall West Indian strode out to bat, he received a standing ovation all the way to the wicket. The ovation lasted longer than his innings, in fact, as he made a duck, but was given another standing ovation all the way back to the pavilion.

NICE TRIP?

DALE LARSON caught his shoe spikes on the steps of the club bar at Indianhead Golf Club in Wisconsin and fell so badly that he broke his jaw and caused untold damage to his teeth. At the time Larson was a little worse for wear, having sufficient alcohol for his blood-alcohol level to suggest he was close to comatose. But nevertheless he sued the club and won over $50,000 in damages. The appeals court judge decided he would have fallen even if he had been stone cold sober.

SORRY MA'AM

JOCKEY TURNED AUTHOR DICK FRANCIS was the unfortunate rider of Devon Loch in 1956. The Queen Mother's horse was clear of the field and just yards from the finish when it leaped into the air without reason and hit the ground on its belly, allowing others to pass.

KNEESY DOES IT

THOMAS MUSTER, the world's number one player for a spell in 1996, had his knee smashed by a drunk driver in 1989, but he worked his way back to fitness by practising from a specially made seat which allowed him to hit strokes even though his leg was encased in plaster.

> **"My golf game's gone off so much that when I went fishing a couple of weeks ago my first cast missed the lake."**
> BEN CRENSHAW

I'm not going to be cox again if I don't get a medal.

Smokin!

"There's no place like home. Scunthorpe United celebrated their 1000th home league game last Saturday. Unfortunately they lost 1-0 to Walsall, but that will come as no surprise to Iron die-hards. United lost their 200th home league game 2-0, their 400th 3-1, their 500th 2-1, their 750th 6-1."

THE GUARDIAN

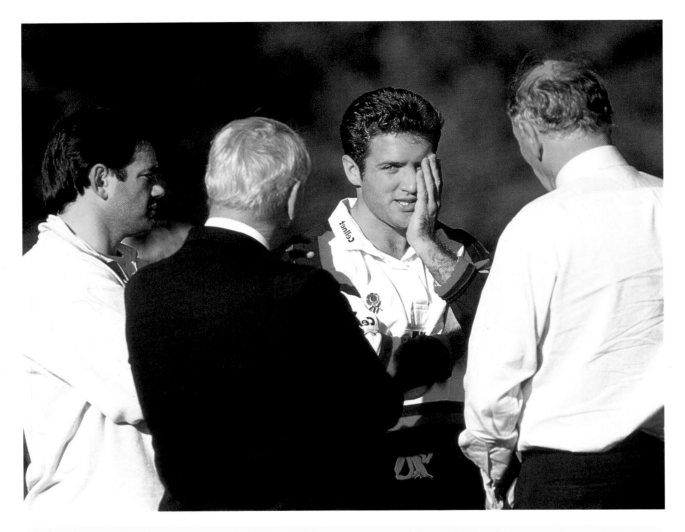

"He's standing next to you, you silly old fart."

BOXING

CRY BABIES

GIVEN THE PENCHANT for modern boxers to cry at the big fight (Mike Tyson before it, Oliver McCall before, during and after) perhaps the sport should revert to its old name in the days of bareknuckle fighting. It was called "The Fancy".

AND ACTION!

BOXING was the first sport to be filmed. A six round fight between Mike Leonard and Jack Cushing was filmed at Edison Labs, New Jersey in 1894.

The one camera was not able to move, so the ring had to be made smaller to accommodate its limited field of vision. Leonard knocked out Cushing in the last round and said afterwards: "I generally hit him in the face because I felt sorry for his family and thought I would select the only place that couldn't be disfigured."

GIVING UP THE GHOST

PANKRATION was an early form of boxing, although more like boxing and wrestling combined in reality. There were few rules, effectively it was anything goes. In 546 BC Arrachian of Phigalia won the Olympic title due to his opponent having "given up". His opponent was actually dead.

BEST JOB I EVER HAD...

LENNOX LEWIS was paid £4 million not to fight Mike Tyson in 1996.

UNFAIR FIGHT

A 1993 WBA light welterweight title fight between Juan Martin Coggi and Eder Gonzalez showed the less honest face of boxing. Two different rounds were ended early to save defending champion Coggi from certain defeat. Referee Isidoro Rodriguez even got involved and held Gonzalez back when Coggi could have been finished off, and at the times when the referee wasn't doing his best to keep Gonzalez away from the stricken Coggi, then his trainer also did his best to hinder the challenger. Eventually Coggi retained the title, but referee Rodriguez and the timekeeper were banned for life.

‘Don King is one of the great humanitarians of our time. He has risen above that great term, prejudice. He has screwed everybody he has ever been around. Hog, dog or frog, it don't matter to Don. If you got a quarter, he wants the first 26 cents.’

RANDALL 'TEX' COBB

CAUGHT SHORT

THE FIRST world title fight held in Austria for many years lasted just 19 seconds, a period of time which also included the count of 10. Defending champion Daniel Jiminez needed just one punch to make local hero Harold Geier see stars.

**Joe Frazier:
'He's so ugly they ought
to donate his face to the
World Wildlife Fund.'**
MUHAMMAD ALI.

53

Excuse Me, Madam?

SEX TESTING of female entrants was introduced into the Olympics in 1968, although a few athletes may well have slipped thought the net prior to that.

In the 1936 Olympics Dora Ratjeu of Germany finished fourth in the Women's High Jump but was subsequently found to be a man.

Polish athlete Eva Klobukowska won two medals at the 1964 Games, a gold and a bronze, but she failed a sex test in 1967.

At the 1976 Olympics in Montreal, Princess Anne was the only female athlete who did not have to undergo a sex test.

'If they kiss him again, those shorts will never hold'

> **"The first time I played The Masters I was so nervous I drank a bottle of rum before I teed off. I shot the happiest 83 of my life."**
>
> CHI CHI RODRIGUEZ.

IS THAT WITH AN 'S'?

WBF SUPERFLYWEIGHT title winner in 1994 was Thailand's Samson Elite Gym. His ring name certainly made life for journalists a lot easier as the new champ's real name was SAENMUANGNOI LOOKCHAOPORMAHESAK.

TROUBLING THE SCORERS

AUSTRALIAN BATSMAN JOHN DYSON carried his bat through the Australian XI's second innings against South Africa in a match in Johannesburg in 1986. Nothing too rare in that, apart from the fact Dyson only scored 18, as the Australian's mustered a total of 61. Dyson's contribution is positively Herculean compared to that of Reg Barlow of Lancashire, who in 1882 against Nottinghamshire, carried his bat in a team total of 69. Barlow's not out contribution was 5.

BUT WE WERE SUPPOSED TO PLAY MIXED FOURSOMES TOMORROW

LADIES GOLF goes back quite a way in time - to Mary Queen of Scots in fact. At the trial that sanctioned her beheading, one of the charges put to her was her complete indifference to the death of her husband Darnley, who was murdered in Edinburgh. It was pointed out that Mary was in fact back on the golf course just a few days after his death.

WATCH THE BIRDIE

THE 1900 OLYMPIC GAMES in Paris featured, for the only time in the Games' history, the event of Live Pigeon Shooting. The gold medal was won by Leon de Lunden of Belgium who killed 21 birds.

SHORT ROLL OF HONOUR

WHEN it comes to living off past glories, Haiti have to look back a long way to wallow in the nostalgic glow of their finest Olympic achievement. It came in 1928, courtesy of Silvio Cator, who won the long jump silver, Haiti's only Olympic medal to date.

MONEY TALKS

JUST HOW MUCH IS SPORT WORTH? NBC bought the rights for the televising in the USA of the summer Olympics in 2004 and 2008, plus the winter Games of 2006 for a whopping $2.3 billion.

> **"Africa has been deprived of the Olympic Games since it began on the pretext that African countries do not have the necessary infrastructure. After Atlanta, any country can apply to host the games."**
> FRANCE SOIR

NO TIME TO BREATHE

JESSE OWENS, showed in 1935 that he was, without doubt one of the supreme athletes of all time by breaking four world records in the space of just 45 minutes.

Hey guys, I don't mind bonding, but can we get rid of the baton!

I swallowed my medal.

Shucks, winner gets to
marry the referee.

SLOWLY DOES IT

THE BBC Television Sports Department is the main reason why we are able to enjoy slow motion action replays of sporting moments. The Beeb's sporting boffins had the first slow-mo machine running in 1968, at a cost of £60,000.

**"Jesus Saves!
But Pearson nets the
rebound."**
BANNER TRIBUTE TO
MANCHESTER UTD
FORWARD STUART
PEARSON
AT 1977 FA CUP FINAL.

**I gotta tell ya,
he's the best 69
I ever had.**

Dutch Red Cross girls manage to revive Linford Christie.

RUN AWAY

A 1994 WBO Straw weight title fight in Majorca lasted just 90 seconds before challenger Arturo Garcia Mayen decided he couldn't go on. He turned his back on the fight and ran back to the safety of his own corner.

TEMPER TEMPER

MARC ROSSET of Switzerland will have learned to control his temper better. In a Hopman Cup final match, Rosset punched his hand through an advertising board in a fit of pique and was then forced to withdraw because of injury. As a result, Croatia won the Cup.

WHO WANTS TO BOWL NOW?

THE ESSEX TEAM OF 1948 will have good reason to remember their match against the touring Australian team. The Aussies scored a mountainous 721 runs in just six hours of play, a record number of runs in one day.

POPULAR GAME

THE 1950 WORLD CUP FINAL in Brazil between Uruguay and Brazil attracted 199,854 spectators.

NO TIME FOR SANDWICH

IN 1937, Brigadier General Critchley travelled from New York to Southampton on the Queen Mary, and then chartered an aeroplane to fly him to Sandwich for the Amateur Championship. He arrived six minutes late for tee-off time and was disqualified.

TAMPER TAMPER

CLEVELAND INDIANS player Albert Belle was banned for a total of seven games in the 1994 season for bat tampering. He was found to be bolstering his own bats with cork.

Hold on a second, David, the PR is worried we haven't got enough of their boots in the picture.

Editorial Warning
Streaking pictures
seriously increase
your heartbeat

You *gotta* spit in it Naz, they've sponsored the bucket as well.

LEFT-RIGHT-LEFT-RIGHT

RONNIE O'SULLIVAN came under fire for playing shots left handed (he is normally right handed) on the way to thrashing Alain Robidoux at the 1996 World Championship. O'Sullivan was diplomatic afterwards, saying: "I'm better left handed than he is right handed."

THE MAESTRO

MAURICE FLITCROFT is a name that strikes fear into the hearts of the R&A. Flitcroft had never before completed 18 holes in golf, but managed to slip through the net and gain entry in the 1976 Open Championship qualifying competition. After a first round of 121, he withdrew saying "I have no chance of qualifying."

FAIR RESULT

A BARE KNUCKLE championship fight held in France in 1887 was declared a draw as the light began to fade. The two contestants, Jake Kilrain and Jem Smith, had endured 106 rounds.

THANKS RAY

JOURNALISTS in the sporting arena rarely have things their own way when it comes to gaining access to the top stars - and then getting a useful quote even if they do. So Ray Illingworth's comments to Martin Johnson, now of The Independent but then a junior reporter with the Leicester Mercury, could not have been construed as helpful. Illingworth, at the time captain of Leicestershire County Cricket Club took Johnson to one side and said: "If you know nowt about t'bloody game, booger off and write about Leicester City."

> **"The scoreline reflects the fairness of the scoreline."**
> DENIS LAW, TV PUNDIT

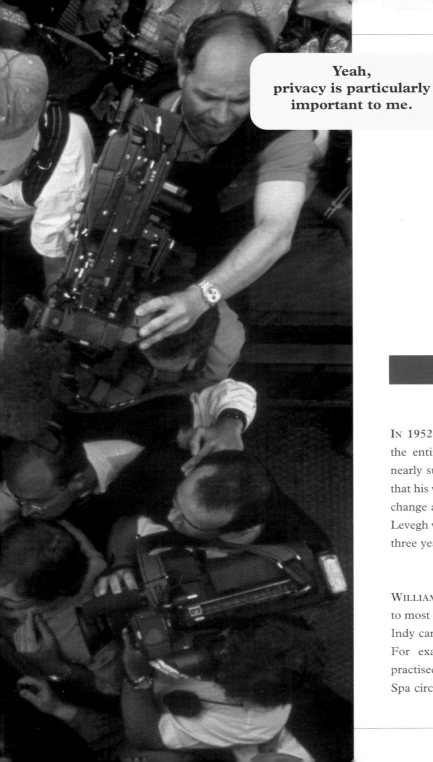

Yeah, privacy is particularly important to me.

MOTOR RACING

TIRED MAN

IN 1952 Frenchman Pierre Levegh attempted to complete the entire 24 hours of Le Mans single-handed and very nearly succeeded. It was only in the 23rd hour of the race that his weariness got the better of him and he missed a gear change and damaged the engine thus forcing him to retire. Levegh was unfortunately killed competing in the same race three years later.

EASY GAME

WILLIAMS Formula One driver Jaques Villeneuve was new to most of the circuits in his fantastic first season away from Indy car racing, but that doesn't mean he wasn't prepared. For example, for the Belgian Grand Prix, Villeneuve practised for hours on a video game featuring the Belgium Spa circuit to get to know the layout.

Damn. Lost it.

"Schumacher is the fastest man on the track. He's going round quicker than anybody else."
MURRAY WALKER

> **"I hit like a mule."**
> MIKE TYSON.

Rare, wild, vicious, stumpy-legged creature walks out with tiger.

74

Please, please, please don't fall on me.

A CHIP OFF THE OLD BLOCK

IT MUST BE IN THE GENES. Liam Botham, son of Ian, took five wickets for 67 runs in his first class debut for Hampshire. The haul included the scalp of Mike Gatting, a wicket his father never took.

ALL CUT UP

1991 OPEN CHAMPION Ian Baker Finch fell on hard times soon after his first and to date only Major Championship triumph. So hard in fact that in the 1995 season he didn't make a single cut in the 18 USPGA Tour events he entered and therefore didn't record a single cent in winnings.

SHORT STORY

GEORGE FOREMAN waited 20 years between world heavyweight titles (1974 to 1994). But apparently he wore the same shorts in each fight.

"I know where the linesman should have put his flag up, and he would have got plenty of help."
RON ATKINSON
DISPUTES A DECISION
AGAINST HIS SIDE.

‘I went to a fight the other night, and an ice hockey game broke out’
RODNEY DANGERFIELD

TENNIS

FIST SERVICE

THE 1983 French Open semi-final between Chris Evert Lloyd and Hanna Mandlikova was halted for a short while in the second set as two spectators set about each other in the stands. A lusty brawl was finally finished with a weighty headbutt and the match continued, with Lloyd winning in three sets.

DARING DODD

LOTTIE DODD holds the distinction of being the first lady tennis player to deliberately display her ankles. She was only 15 when she won her first Wimbledon title in 1887, and that allowed her to get away with wearing a schoolgirl's calf-length dress. Her youth also meant she did not have to wear a corset, an encumbrance which helped slow down her opponents.

LEG IT

AT WIMBLEDON IN 1985, Anne White caused more than a stir when she turned up to play her match against Pam Shriver clad, not in the traditional shirt and skirt, but rather in a figure hugging, all white body stocking which covered her from her ankles up to her neck.

The Wimbledon powers that be were not impressed, and when the match resumed next day, White was wearing more conventional attire.

The Times tennis correspondent, Rex Bellamy, wrote: "Wimbledon did not permit her to wear the same clothing as yesterday. They insisted that she expose her legs, which seem to go on forever but could not honestly be described as boring."

FEELING SLEEPY

WIMBLEDON line judge Dorothy Cavis Brown found fame at the 1964 event. Officiating in the first round match between Clark Graebner and Abe Segal, which was obviously not an exciting game, Cavis Brown nodded off while on duty. It was her first and last Wimbledon as an official.

I *HATE* THESE SHORTS!

Whoa, wait up guys.
This ain't no ordinary ball.
It's growing.

"It's rumoured that a well-known New England newspaper is to sponsor a topless female basketball team - to be called the Boston Globes."

PLAYBOY

TAKE THAT

COLOURFUL CHARACTER Dennis Rodman of the Chicago Bulls was fined a mere $20,000 for headbutting a referee. Rodman earns approximately eight times that amount each week. In the same year, Rodman posed nude for Playboy alongside his stripper wife Stacy Yarborough.

NICE DRESS

DENNIS RODMAN launched his autobiography in 1996, entitled "Bad As I Wanna Be." Rodman attended the book launch wearing make-up and a fetching wedding dress.

BIG LOSER

SINCE starting his NBA coaching career in 1970, Bill Fitch has managed to lose over 1,000 games - he is the first NBA coach to pass the milestone.

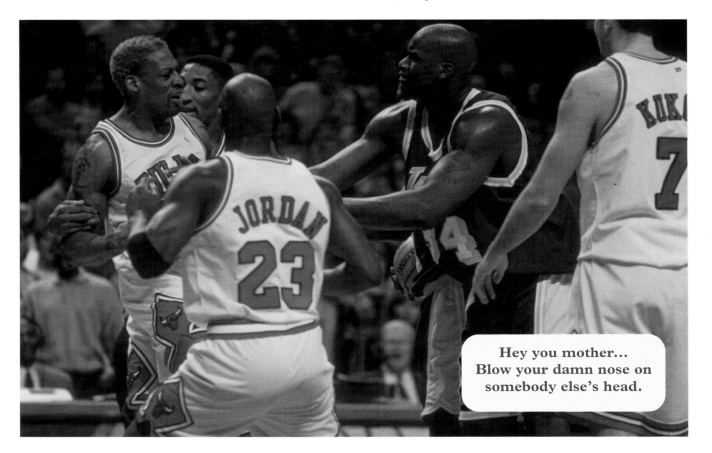

Hey you mother...
Blow your damn nose on
somebody else's head.

WHERE'S THE SEA?

AUSTRIA, Hungary and Switzerland have all won Olympic medals for yachting, despite all being landlocked countries.

SUN STOPS PLAY

A RARE EVENT occurred during the 1995 test match between England and West Indies at Old Trafford.
So bright was the late afternoon sun that it forced an early break for tea. Sunlight reflecting off a glass roof was dazzling the batsmen.

LONG DRIVER

FLOYD ROOD golfed his way across the USA, literally, on a route covering 3,397 miles. The "round" took him 479 days to complete, and he returned a score of 114,737 shots.

"Dennis Lillee comes in, his shirt big enough for two men - if only they could get into the trousers."
JOHN ARLOTT

> **‘Ah, isn't that nice, the wife of the Cambridge President is kissing the cox of the Oxford crew ’**
>
> HARRY CARPENTER

PLAY ON

A 1996 RESERVES MATCH between Norwich City and West Ham was called off by the referee who deemed the pitch unplayable. However, both teams and the fans who had turned up wanted the game to go ahead, so when the original referee had left the ground, a local replacement was found who agreed to take control. West Ham won 3-2.

BUT WE WANTED TO WIN

A 1920 OLYMPIC SUCCESS for the British team against Belgium was tainted by the band refusing to play the National Anthem at the medal ceremony - and officials refused to raise the Union Jack. The games that year were held in Antwerp, Belgium.

"I've never had a hat trick before. I've never bowled three straight deliveries before."
HAMPSHIRE CRICKETER
KEVIN JAMES

"American athletes are bilingual: they speak English and profanity."
GORDIE HOWE

"Look lads, we can piss this game. I already have."

Araldite.

WELL HELD 1

GRAHAM ROOPE'S reputation as being a quality slip fielder is well backed by statistics. During a 22 year cricket career, Roope bagged 602 catches, at an average of 1.49 catches per game. Peter Walker held exactly the same average as Roope for his 16 year career, but Walker managed to hold on to 697 catches.

THE MIGHTY FALL

CRICKET can produce the odd upset. Take the 1996 World Cup when the mighty West Indies lost to Kenya. Perhaps lost isn't the right word, Kenya bowled the Windies out for just 93 runs, so "annihilated" is probably more appropriate.

WHAT'S THE SCORE?

A GOOD JOB Brian Lara didn't come along in the 18th century. Runs scored were recorded by cutting notches in a stick.

WELL HELD 2

A GOLDEN TEST MATCH SPECIAL RADIO MOMENT. Fred Trueman swoops in the commentary box to catch a cake which had tumbled off a monitor, just inches from the floor. The whole incident is covered on air and Trueman is rewarded with applause from his fellow commentators and the congratulatory: "A sensational piece of fielding."

WHO PUT THAT THERE?

FINDING ENOUGH SPACE to play cricket can be a problem in Fiji. In Lana a pitch was moved to make way for building work, and as a result the outfielders found themselves standing in the sea.

ARLOTT'S LAST STAND

WHEN JOHN ARLOTT said his last words as a member of BBC Radio's Test Match Special commentary team, both teams turned towards the commentary position and applauded.

HOME IN TIME FOR TEA

SURREY AND LEICESTERSHIRE contested the shortest ever Sunday league game in 1996. Leicestershire struggled to 48 all out in 22 overs. Surrey knocked off the required runs in just 4.3 overs.

XXXXCEPTIONAL

AUSTRALIAN BATSMAN DAVID BOON once sank 58 cans of lager (provided by the team sponsor) during the flight between Sydney and London.

RED CARDED

SV MANJREKER holds the distinction of being sent off in a cricket match - for using abusive language in a match between Bombay and Maharashtra.

QUICK HICK

GRAEME HICK set a new record in the summer of 1986. Hick amassed a total of 2004 runs for the season, and at the age of 20 years 111 days he became the youngest player ever to do so.

THEY CALL HIM AYLESBURY

MARK ROBINSON of Northants will not lay any claims to being a batsman in the Viv Richards mould. Robinson finished the 1990 season with a batting average of precisely 0.5. At one stage of the season the unfortunate batting bunny managed to record 12 consecutive ducks.

THEY CALL HIM AYLESBURY, TOO

NEW ZEALAND cricketer Danny Morrison, admittedly more of a bowler than a batsman, set a new record in 1996 when he completed his 29th duck in just 69 test innings.

FANCY A FAG?

PHIL TUFNELL found himself centre of controversy, not for the first time, during England's 1997 tour of New Zealand. The left arm spinner was accused of smoking marijuana in a Christchurch restaurant, which he denied. Although he did choose the Oasis song "Cigarettes and Alcohol" as the tune which he would be greeted with over the tannoy each time he walked out to bat.

"The best and fairest of all umpires. Great bloke, completely bonkers."

IAN BOTHAM'S TRIBUTE TO THE RETIRING DICKIE BIRD

THE RACE
THAT NEVER WAS

THE COMBINATION of race horse Esha Ness, ridden by John White, thought they had reached the pinnacle of achievement in national hunt racing when they were first past the post in the 1993 Grand National. Already halted due to a false start, the race never got going officially as the second start was also declared false. Unfortunately, starter and flag man were unable to communicate the message to all the field and several horses completed the whole race. White went from the top of the world to the depths of despair within a few seconds of crossing the finishing line. He didn't ride another Grand National.

DOPEY

THE JOCKEY CLUB announced in 1994 that it was to begin random drug testing. The list of banned substances is actually quite short for reasons explained by Chief Medical Officer Michael Turner: "We're not looking for performance enhancing drugs."

ALLITERATION'S ALL YOU NEED

IN THE GRAND NATIONAL of 1928 there were just two finishers: Tipperary Tim and Billy Barton.

MAGNIFICENT SEVEN

FRANKIE DETTORI set the racing world alight in 1996 by riding seven winners in seven races at Ascot. the combined odds for the feat worked out at 25,095-1.

> ‘A race horse is the only animal that can take several thousand people for a ride at the same time ’
>
> ANON.

WHAT'S FOR TEA?

JACK BANNISTER promised he would eat his words if South Africa beat England in the 1995/96 test series. South Africa won, Bannister duly tucked into a meal of newsprint.

FLY BY

MARTIN BRUNDLE had an amazing escape from a spectacular crash at Melbourne in the 1996 Australian Grand Prix. Brundle's Jordan clipped another car at the first turn of the race, and then somersaulted over several more cars before disintegrating on impact with the ground. Brundle not only emerged unscathed from the wreckage, but ran all the way back to the pit lane to get the spare Jordan car for the restart of the race.

Brundle said afterwards: "I thought the last two rolls were unnecessary. I'd got the message by then." Fellow driver David Coulthard, who watched Brundle fly over his own car, remarked: "I thought Martin was dead."

Brundle still didn't finish the race, he spun out in the spare car.

But it's the rules, Rosita. If there is a false start you have to run the race again; even the marathon.

‘All I want to do is hit somebody in the mouth. It's a whole lot easier than working for a living.’

RANDALL COBB

Here come the Brits.

"The worst thing about playing for Great Britain is the sleeveless shirts. It means you have to shave your armpits before every game."
HOCKEY PLAYER
KAREN BROWN.

FANCY A BET?

BETTING ON FOOTBALL can be a lucrative business if you get it right. Jim Wright bagged £654,375 in 1992 having staked a £1000 each way treble on forecasting the winners of League Divisions 1, 2 and 3. Newcastle, Stoke and Cardiff, respectively, did Mr Wright the biggest favour of his life.

"I'm 49, I've had a brain haemorrhage and a triple bypass and I could still go out and play a reasonable game of rugby union. But I wouldn't last 30 seconds in rugby league."

FORMER WIGAN COACH GRAHAM LOWE

"Golfers don't fist fight. They cuss a bit. But they wouldn't punch anything or anybody. They might hurt their hands and have to change their grip."

DAN JENKINS

COSTLY WAGER

BETTING ON FOOTBALL can also be painful if you get it wrong. Witness the case of a Malaysian who staked a total of £242,000 on Mexico to beat Bulgaria and Brazil to beat Italy in 90 minutes at the World Cup 1994. Oops! Neither bet came up.

Say Al, you can see
why women go for us
huh?

AMERICAN FOOTBALL II

TAKE TWO

DOES TELEVISION hold too much sway in sport? In the USA it is not an unknown phenomenon for an American Football match to be restarted because the TV crew had missed the kick-off first time around.

NEVER BROKE SWEAT

CHICAGO BEARS quarterback Bobby Douglas enjoyed a high reward for little effort in a 1973 game. He scored four touchdowns in the match, but only had to run a total of five yards to achieve the feat.

OUCH!

LA RAIDERS Hall of Fame player Jim Otto finally quit the game in 1974, when injuries got the better of him. The list of Otto's ailments was not a short one: 10 broken noses, a broken jaw, six operations on his right leg and three on his left being the highlights.

"I can't win with this bunch of stiffs."
COACH BUDDY PARKER WALKS OUT ON PITTSBURGH STEELERS AFTER EIGHT YEARS IN THE JOB.

"I don't know. I never smoked Astroturf."
JOE NAMATH, NEW YORK JETS, WHEN ASKED WHETHER HE PREFERED ASTROTURF TO GRASS.

'It isn't necessary to see a good tackle. You can hear it.'
KNUTE ROCKNE

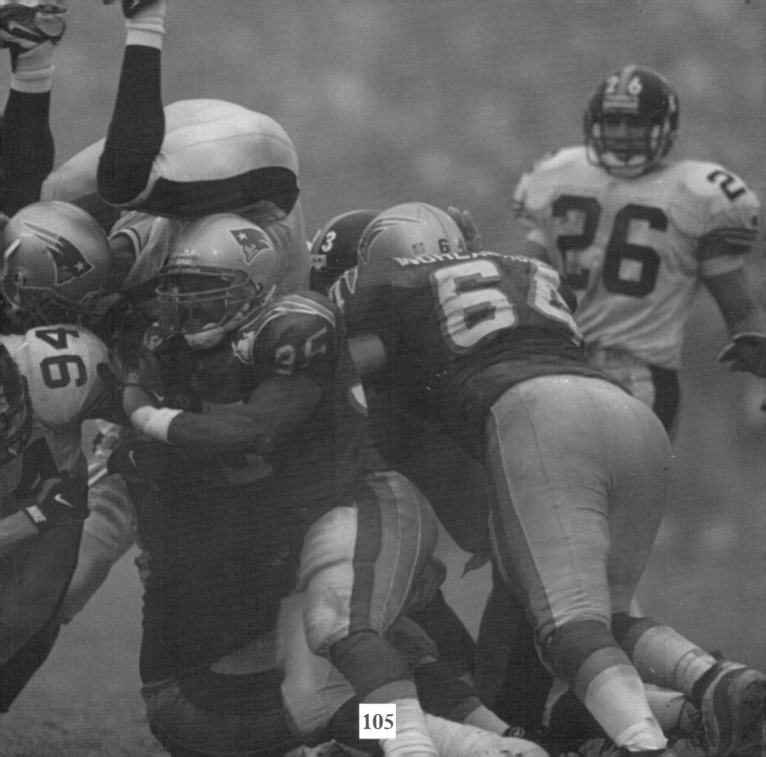

‘A puck is a hard rubber disk that hockey players strike when they can't hit one another.’

JIM CANNON

SQUID STOPS PLAY

A MATCH IN SOUTH AFRICA between Border and Boland was reportedly brought to a halt due to "fried calamari".

Batsman Darrel Cullinan, on his way to 78 not out, smashed a six which landed in a frying pan, where aforementioned calamari were cooking. It was 10 minutes before the ball was cool enough for umpires to remove the coat of grease, and even then the ball was too slippy for bowlers to hold and had to be replaced.

BUT, DAD!

THE 1908 OLYMPIC MIDDLEWEIGHT FINAL was not without controversy. John Douglas of Britain beat Reg Baker of Australia to take the gold. But Baker complained that the referee had not been impartial. He had a point, the ref was the father of Douglas.

SELF DEFENCE

OLYMPIC JUDO GOLD MEDALLIST in 1976 Hector Rodriguez attributed his success on the mat to his six older brothers. He took up judo to protect himself from them.

ONE SIDED

The highest score recorded in an international hockey match occurred in 1923 when India beat USA 24-1.

ANYONE FOR TENNIS?

TENNIS STAR IVAN LENDL made his professional debut as a golfer in the 1996 Czech Open. He found it tough going, though, shooting an 11 over par 83 in the first round.

I'M A MAN NOW

AUSTRALIAN DAVID DICKS became the youngest person to sail solo around the world non-stop. He celebrated his 18th birthday during the 264 day voyage.

REVENGE IS SWEET

A GOOSE basking in the sun by a lake in Massachusetts took umbrage at being hit by a golf ball. It kicked the ball into the water by way of revenge.

"The British press hate a winner who's British. They don't like any British man to have balls as big as a cow's like I have."

BOXER NIGEL BENN

"Being dropped and Take That splitting up on the same day is enough to finish anyone off."

ENGLAND RUGBY PLAYER MARTIN BAYFIELD

"Gazza is no longer a fat, drunken imbecile...he is in fact a football genius."

THE DAILY MIRROR PROFFERS AN APOLOGY DURING EURO 96.

TIN POTTY

Harry Dearth once competed in a match play game at Bushey Hall while wearing a full suit of armour. He lost 2&1.

BIG HITTER

BOMBARDIER BILLY WELLS, heavyweight champion of Britain, was the first man to hit the gong which the Rank Organisation began using to open its productions in 1935.

"You have to have six O-levels to understand them all."
WIGAN PLAYER SHAUN EDWARDS ON RUGBY UNION RULES.

Then her face lit up as her fingertips at last brushed up against the hidden key to the strange native chastity belt.

Time to unwind for the senior product-test inspector at inflatable sex toy factory.

IF YOU ENJOYED THIS BOOK, WHAT ABOUT THESE!

All these books are available at your local book shop or can be ordered direct from the publisher.
Just list the titles you require and give your name address, including post code.
Prices and availability are subject to change without notice.

Please send to Chameleon Cash Sales, 106 Great Russell Street London WCIB 3LJ, a cheque or postal order for £7.99 and add the following for postage and packaging:

UK - £1.00 For the first book. 50p for the second and 30p for the third for each additional book up to a maximum of £3.00.
OVERSEAS -(including Eire) £2.00 For the first book and £1.00 for the second and 50p for each additional book up to a maximum of £3.00.